First Science Experiments

MAGNET POWER!

by Shar Levine and Leslie Johnstone

illustrations by Steve Harpster

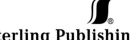

Sterling Publishing Co., Inc.
New York

For my wonderful nephews, El'ad and Tamir—SL

For Emily and Kyle Sharf—LJ

Library of Congress Cataloging-in-Publication Data

Levine, Shar, 1953-
    First science experiments. Magnet power! / Shar Levine and Leslie Johnstone;
illustrated by Steve Harpster.
        p. cm.
    Includes index.
    ISBN-13: 978-1-4027-2438-1
    ISBN-10: 1-4027-2438-1
    1. Magnets—Experiments—Juvenile literature. I. Johnstone, Leslie.
II. Harpster, Steve, ill. III. Title.

QC757.5.L48 2006
538—dc22

                                    2005037678

10 9 8 7 6 5 4 3 2 1

Published by Sterling Publishing Co., Inc.
387 Park Avenue South, New York, NY 10016
© 2006 by Shar Levine and Leslie Johnstone
Distributed in Canada by Sterling Publishing
℅ Canadian Manda Group, 165 Dufferin Street
Toronto, Ontario, Canada M6K 3H6
Distributed in Great Britain by GMC Distribution Services
Castle Place, 166 High Street, Lewes, East Sussex, England BN7 1XU
Distributed in Australia by Capricorn Link (Australia) Pty. Ltd.
P.O. Box 704, Windsor, NSW 2756, Australia

Sterling ISBN-13: 978-1-4027-2438-1
        ISBN-10: 1-4027-2438-1

For information about custom editions, special sales, premium and
corporate purchases, please contact Sterling Special Sales
Department at 800-805-5489 or specialsales@sterlingpub.com.

Contents

Note to Parents and Teachers

There are few things in the world more interesting to a young child than a magnet. Playing with magnets is a simple and relatively safe activity that can entertain a child for hours, even days. Magnets make science magic. They can pick up some things, but not others. They can move objects, by either pushing or pulling them. They can even work under water. This book is designed to answer very basic questions young children have about magnets.

If your child wants to learn more about a specific topic, you can visit the library or surf the Web. Think of the things you will discover together.

Be Safe

We have tried to make the activities as safe and as simple as possible. Some adult supervision is needed with small children, especially when performing experiments that involve anything sharp. Please read the following rules with your child before starting any activity.

Do

✔ Ask an adult to read through an activity with you before you begin.

✔ Have an adult handle all sharp objects.

✔ Keep your work area clean and put things away afterward.

✔ Keep magnets and supplies away from young children and pets.

✔ Tell an adult immediately if anyone is hurt in any way.

✔ Wash your hands after performing all experiments.

✔ Store your magnets as shown on page 7.

Don't

✔ Don't use your magnets near computer equipment or software. Keep them away from TVs and stereos, video and audio tapes, video games, MP3 players or minidiscs, watches, anything digital, or with a magnetic strip, such as a bank or library card.

✔ Never put magnets and other experiment materials or supplies into your mouth.

✔ Don't drop magnets or let them snap together. When separating them, don't slide one across the other. Ask an adult to pry the two magnets apart.

Introduction

In this book you will learn all about a kind of North and South Pole without polar bears or penguins. But you'll find out why magnets are so "cool," and you won't even have to wear gloves to keep your hands toasty. You will need several different kinds of magnets for the activities in this book. Some magnets are sold in sets that include: bar, horseshoe, circular, and stick magnets, and a bag of filings. You can usually find other inexpensive magnets at toy, discount, hardware, or craft stores. You don't need to buy powerful, expensive magnets for these children's experiments. Science museum shops also carry magnets, and you can find some on-line. We do suggest that you avoid N.I.B.—Neodymium–Iron–Boron (NdFeB)—supermagnets, as they break or chip easily and can be a danger in the hands of young children.

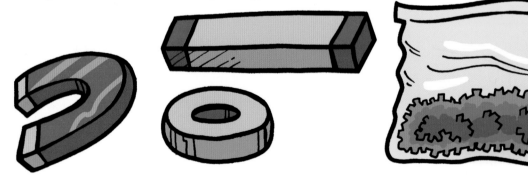

Storing your magnets

If you have a favorite toy, you might keep it in a special place so it won't get broken. Magnets may not seem that fragile, but you do need to take care when you put them away. Here's how to store a magnet:

❶ Place the opposite poles of the magnets next to each other (north to south and south to north) and store in pairs.

❷ If your magnets have keepers or small pieces of metal that fit across the poles, always put them on the magnets after you have finished your experiments.

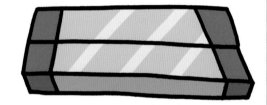

❸ Do not drop the magnets, or bang them against anything hard.

❹ Keep the magnets someplace cool. Do not expose them to high temperatures.

❺ Do not store a magnet near your compass.

What do the N and the S on a magnet mean?

Some magnets, usually those shaped like bars or horseshoes, have N or S on each end. Circular magnets, shaped like donuts, don't have anything painted on them. But what do the N and S mean?

You need

- 2 bar magnets
- masking tape
- about 18 inches (46 cm) of string
- table

Do this

1. Loop the string around the middle of a magnet and knot it in place. Center the loop so the magnet hangs parallel to the floor. Tape the loop string to the magnet to hold it in place.

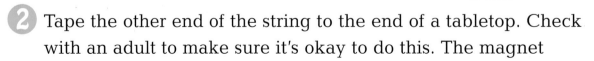

2. Tape the other end of the string to the end of a tabletop. Check with an adult to make sure it's okay to do this. The magnet

should be hanging over the side of the table, suspended from the loop of string. It should be able to move freely.

3 Hold the second magnet and slowly bring the N side close to the N on the hanging magnet. What happens?

4 Turn the magnet around and bring the S side close to the N on the hanging magnet. Which way does the hanging magnet move?

5 Try this again, this time bringing the S side close to the S on the hanging magnet. What happens now?

What happened?

When you held the N side close to the N side of the hanging magnet, the hanging magnet moved away. The same thing happened when you held the two S sides together. When you held the N side towards the S side of the hanging magnet, the magnets moved together. The N on a magnet means North or North-seeking, while the S means South or South-seeking. When magnets pull towards each other it means they are attracted; when they push away from each other it means they are repelled. The opposite sides of magnets, or north and south poles, always attract or pull towards each other. The same sides of magnets, or north and north or south and south, always repel or push away from each other.

Where can I find magnets ?

If you wanted to look for a magnet, where would you search? You might find a magnet in the back of your drawer or the bottom of your toy box. Do you think you could find a magnet outdoors?

You need

- strong bar or horseshoe magnet
- lodestone (piece of magnetite)
- 2 sealable plastic bags
- rock collection
- sand
- small shovel

Do this

 Next time you are at the beach, bring along a bar magnet or lodestone (available from museum stores or online). Place it in a plastic bag and swirl the bag in the sand. Do any small dark bits of sand stick to the bag? Collect these bits in a clean sealable bag.

2 Visit a museum or science store and see if they have any of the following samples: magnetite, hematite, pyrite, silicon, galena, tiger eye, bismuth, franklinite, solalite, jasper, or quartz. Hold your magnet or lodestone near these rocks. Can you feel a weak attraction?

3 Dig around in your garden. Place a magnet in a plastic bag and see if you can attract any small bits of magnetic material that might be in the soil.

What happened?

Sand in many places around the world contains small bits of a magnetic mineral called magnetite. If any bits of sand were attracted to your magnet, they probably contained this mineral. You may also have found a very weak attraction between the magnet and other minerals, such as hematite and franklinite.

Did You Know?

The word "magnetite" comes from the Greek word Magnes, meaning "stones from Magnesia." Magnesia was a place in Asia Minor where lots of magnetite was found.

What can a magnet pick up?

You've seen how a magnet can attract or repel another magnet, but what other kinds of things will a magnet pick up? It's time to play some magnetic hide-and-seek.

You need

- magnet
- your toy box
- small box of steel paper clips
- marbles
- coins
- paper
- adult helper

Do this

1. Have an adult help you gather items for testing. Make sure you never hold your magnet next to any of the items listed in the Don'ts list on page 5.

2. Hold your magnet close to some of your toys. Which toys are attracted to the magnet? Which toys are not attracted?

3 Hold your magnet close to other metallic objects such as paper clips, coins, jewelry, hair clips, screws and nuts, spoons, pens, desks, filing cabinets, drawer handles. Which objects were attracted by the magnet?

4 Hold your magnet close to nonmetallic objects such as pencils, plastic containers, drinking glasses, plates, windows, wooden shelves, books. Is the magnet attracted to any of these things?

What happened?

Your magnet was attracted to many metallic objects, such as small toy cars, paper clips, and some kinds of coins. These objects were made of materials such as iron, nickel, cobalt, or mixtures of these metals such as steel. The magnet did not attract some metallic objects, such as gold jewelry and copper pennies. Even though you couldn't pick up the handle of a drawer or door with your magnet, you could still feel the attraction between the two objects if it contained a magnetic metal. Your magnet did not attract any nonmetallic objects.

How can you stop a magnet from picking up objects ?

It's fun to pick up objects with a magnet, but what if you didn't want it to attract an object? Can you stop the force of magnetic attraction?

You will need

- bar magnet
- box of steel paper clips
- piece of cardboard
- book cover
- thin computer mouse pad

- plastic lid
- paper
- metal frying pan
- T-shirt

Do this

1. Place an open box of paper clips on a table. Hold a bar magnet over the clips. How many can the magnet pick up?

2. Return the clips to the box and shake it. Place a plastic lid over the clips and hold the magnet over the lid. Lift the lid and magnet. Were any paper clips attracted to the magnet through the lid?

3 Try it using cardboard instead of plastic. What happened?

4 Repeat step 2, each time using a different material: book cover, sheet of paper, mouse pad, T-shirt—whatever you have. Does the magnet still attract the clips through these objects?

5 Place the magnet in a metal frying pan or pot. Hold the pan with the magnet over the paper clips. What happens now?

What happened?

When the material or object between the magnet and the paper clips was very thin, the magnet could still attract the clips. While you can't see it, there is something called a magnetic field. This field goes outward from the ends of the magnet and allows magnets to attract things they are not touching. The magnetic field can pass through materials such as paper and cloth if they aren't too thick. The field can change directions when it moves through such materials as metals. When the magnet was placed in the pot, the pot changed the direction of the magnetic field so that the field wasn't strong enough on the other side of the pot to attract the clips.

What is the smallest magnet ?

Your magnets are a good size for experiments. Some magnets are large enough to pick up a car! But how small can a magnet be?

You need

♦ plastic tweezers
♦ iron filings
♦ thin plastic tube or straw
♦ modeling clay
♦ bar magnet
♦ compass
♦ adult helper

Do this

1. Use tweezers to pick up a single piece of iron filing. Hold it close to the other iron filings. Does this piece attract other filings?

2. Have an adult use modeling clay to seal one end of a plastic tube straw. The adult should fill the tube near to the top with iron filings and seal that end of the tube. Be careful that the modeling clay doesn't fall out the ends.

3 Using only one end of the bar magnet, stroke the tube in one direction only. Do this for about 25 strokes.

4 Place a compass flat on a table or the floor. Hold the tube over the compass. Does the needle move towards the tube? Move the tube in a circle over the compass. What happens to the needle?

5 Shake the tube several times and repeat step 4. What happens to the compass needle now?

What happened?

Each tiny iron filing became a magnet with a north and a south pole. The filings didn't move much when you stroked them, but the bar magnet lined up tiny magnetic regions of the filings, called domains. The filings then acted like a magnet and attracted the magnetic needle of the compass. After you shook up the tube, the domains of the iron filings pointed in various directions again.

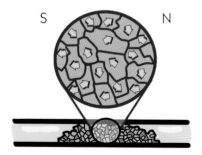
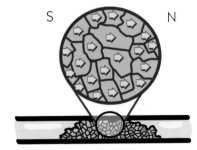

Can I make something magnetic?

There's only one magnet available and you and your best friend both want to do the experiments in this book? The store is closed so you can't buy another one. What's a kid to do?

You need

- ◆ bar magnet
- ◆ steel knitting needle
- ◆ steel paper clips
- ◆ section of metal clothes hanger or soft iron nail

Do this

1. Touch the knitting needle to the paper clips. Are any attracted to the needle?

2. Hold the knitting needle and stroke one end of the bar magnet from the top of the needle straight down to the bottom. Do not go back and forth; stroke in only one direction for several minutes.

3 Touch the needle to the paper clips. Do any stick to the needle after stroking it?

4 Try this again, using a metal hanger or soft iron nail. Remember to place the clips in the box and shake it before each activity.

What happened?

You've created a spare magnet. The knitting needle is only a magnet temporarily, and it's not as strong as your bar magnet. How does rubbing the needle turn it into a magnet? Remember the iron filings activity (pages 16–17)? At first the filings in the tube were all jumbled. Stroking a magnet near the filings caused them to line up in one direction. It's the same with the needle. Rubbing metal won't always create a magnet. The material must be ferromagnetic.

Domain Theory

When ferromagnetic materials, such as iron, are placed in contact with strong magnets they can become magnetic themselves. Microscopic sections of the metal, called magnetic domains, line up so they have a north and a south pole. When enough domains point in the same direction, the metal becomes a magnet.

Does a magnet ever lose its power?

Now that you know you can make something magnetic, will it always stay this way?

You need

- ♦ magnetized steel knitting needle
- ♦ bar magnet
- ♦ steel paper clips
- ♦ piece of carpet or thick towel

Do this

1 Magnetize a steel knitting needle by rubbing the needle in one direction with a strong magnet (see pages 18–19).

2 Dip your needle into some paper clips to make sure it attracts them. Place the clips back in the box and shake the box.

3 Hold the knitting needle by one end and smack the needle hard against the carpet or into a thick towel. Do this several times, hitting the needle as hard as you can against the material.

4 Dip your needle into the paper clips again. How many clips were attracted to the needle this time?

What happened?

The magnetized knitting needle attracted the paper clips, but after the needle was dropped it lost its ability to pick up the clips. When you stroked the knitting needle with the magnet, you made the magnetic domains in the knitting needle line up: the north poles of the domains all faced the same way, and the south poles faced in the opposite direction. By hitting the knitting needle against something, you caused the magnetic domains to become mixed up or random again, so they lost their magnetism and couldn't attract the steel paper clips.

Where is the largest magnet in the world?

Look down. You are standing on the world's largest magnet. No, it's not in your home, or even in your city. It is the Earth. Believe it or not, the Earth is a giant magnet, with a north pole (at the South Pole) and a south pole (at the North Pole). Confused? That's okay! Try this, to learn more.

You need

- compass
- plastic lid
- modeling clay
- bar magnet

Do this

1 Roll a ball of modeling clay and flatten it into a dome shape on the plastic lid. Place this on a table. Push the N end of a bar magnet into the clay so that it stands upright.

2 Hold a compass between your fingers and, beginning at the top of the bar magnet, move your compass around the magnet.

Watch what happens to the needle on the magnet as you move your hand around an imaginary globe.

What happened?

Chances are you are really confused. Why did you put the bar magnet in the clay so that the south pole was on top and the north pole was on the bottom? The N on a compass, and on a magnet, stands for north-seeking. Remember (page 9)? This means that it will be attracted to the opposite pole. The magnetic field around the Earth is similar to the field around the magnet you placed in the clay. If you were to walk from near the Earth's North Pole to near its South Pole, the north needle of your compass would always point towards the north.

Did You Know?

North may not always be north to a magnet. Over hundreds and hundreds of years the magnetic field of the Earth changes direction. This change is very slow, so we may never see it change, but rock samples on the Earth show that it has changed several times in the past. At one time, the South Pole was actually a magnetic south pole, not a magnetic north pole as it is today.

How can a magnet help me if I get lost?

Today, if a car has a GPS (Global Positioning System), its computer screen shows you right where you are. But how did early explorers ever find their way to new places and continents.

You need

♦ compass

Do this

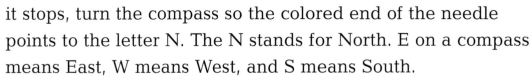

1 Place the compass on a flat, nonmetallic surface. Watch the needle rotate, moving in a circle. When it stops, turn the compass so the colored end of the needle points to the letter N. The N stands for North. E on a compass means East, W means West, and S means South.

2 Hold the compass out on your flat palm. Turn around slowly and watch the compass needle as you move. What happens to the colored end of the needle?

What happened?

As you turned, the colored end of the compass needle always pointed in the same direction: North. The compass needle is magnetic. One end is attracted to the North, so the other end points South. But where is the magnet? It's the Earth! Our planet acts like a giant magnet with north and south poles. That's why the compass needle points in the same direction as the magnetic field.

Did You Know?

Some animals seem to have a built-in compass, or at least a very good sense of direction. Birds always fly south for the winter. Monarch butterflies also migrate, going not only south but back to the very same place every year. In northern Australia, termites build tall, flat, magnetic mounds parallel to each other. The mounds' magnetic fields all point in the same north/south direction.

What happens if I don't have a compass and I'm lost? How do I find my way

Using a compass to help you find which way is north is simple, now that you know how to use a compass. But what if you don't have a compass? Can you make your own?

You need

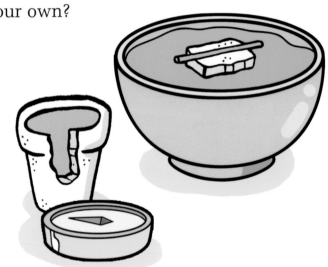

- ◆ steel paper clip
- ◆ flat surface
- ◆ bar magnet
- ◆ bowl
- ◆ water
- ◆ disposable foam cup
- ◆ compass (optional)

Do this

1. Straighten a paper clip and lay it on a nonmetallic surface.

2. Hold down one end of the straightened clip. Stroke the clip in one direction only with the bar magnet. Do this about 25 times.

3 Break off a small, flat piece from the bottom of the foam cup and place the wire on this piece.

4 Fill a bowl or container with water and gently float the section of foam cup with the magnetized clip in the middle.

5 Place a compass on the table next to the bowl of water. Compare the direction the magnetized clip is pointing to the direction the compass is pointing. Are they both pointing in the same direction?

What happened?

The magnetized clip behaved just like the compass. It turned so that one end faced north. Like a life jacket, the section of foam cup helped the paper clip stay afloat. The water allowed the clip to move and align itself with the Earth's magnetic field. The Vikings didn't have compasses. Instead, they floated lodestones in water to help them find their way to new lands.

If I were at the North Pole, where would my compass point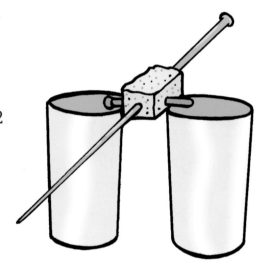

That's a good question! You won't need to set out on a polar expedition to learn the answer, either.

You need

- ◆ adult helper
- ◆ long steel knitting needle
- ◆ plastic foam block, about 2 by 2 by 3 inches (5 by 5 by 8 cm)
- ◆ short knitting needle (metal)
- ◆ 2 tall glasses or jars (same height)
- ◆ bar magnet

Do this

1. Ask your helper to push the long needle down the center of the block, through the longest side. Place the block halfway down the needle. Now the short needle must be pushed through the foam so the two needles cross, as shown. The long needle is called a dip needle.

2 Place the ends of the shorter needle between two tall glasses and balance the dip needle. The long knitting needle should be parallel, or even, with the tabletop.

3 Lift the dip needle from the glasses. Starting from the block outward, stroke the long needle with the N side of a bar magnet about 25 times. Only stroke in one direction—not back and forth.

4 Next, start from the other side of the block. Moving outward, stroke the needle with the S side about 25 times in one direction.

5 Place the dip needle back between the glasses. What happens?

What happened?

After magnetizing the needle, it dipped or tipped downward. It behaved like a magnet and was attracted to something. But what? The magnetic field of the Earth. Use a protractor to measure how far the needle has dipped where you are.

At North Pole   At South Pole   At Equator

Does a magnet have to touch something to pick it up ?

You've seen how thick materials can stop a magnet from attracting objects, but is it possible for a magnet not to touch anything and still pick it up? Let's see.

You need

♦ bar magnet
♦ metal knitting needle
♦ soft iron nail
♦ steel paper clips

Do this

1. Place the paper clips on a wooden table or on the floor.

2. Touch the clips with the knitting needle. Do any paper clips stick to the knitting needle? Try it again, this time using the nail. Did any paper clips stick to the nail?

3. Touch the knitting needle to the clips again, but this time hold the bar magnet just above the opposite end of the needle. Did any clips stick to the needle? Move the magnet closer to the needle until the paper clips are attracted to the needle.

4. Take the magnet away from the needle. What happens?

5. Turn the magnet around and point the opposite pole toward the end of the needle. What happens to the clips?

6. Repeat steps 2 to 5, using the nail.

What happened?

The needle and nail didn't attract any paper clips until you held a magnet near their ends, then something unexpected happened. The metal objects attracted the clips. The clips still attracted the metal objects after the magnet was taken away because the domains in the metal objects had lined up in one direction. This made them into temporary magnets. When you turned the magnet around, the clips very quickly fell off. The magnet changed the poles of the needle and nail. When same-seeking poles are placed together (in this case the needle and the clips) they repel each other.

How can I see something that is invisible ?

Hold a magnet in your hand. You know it's there, but can you see any lines coming from the magnet? As hard as you look you can't, because the magnet's lines of force are invisible. Fear not, help is on the way.

You need

- ◆ adult helper
- ◆ iron filings
- ◆ clear, flat plastic container, about 6 by 8 inches (15 by 20 cm)
- ◆ plastic wrap
- ◆ masking tape
- ◆ different kinds of magnets

Do this

1 Have an adult add about ¼ cup (60 mL) of iron filings to the flat container. Close it with a clear lid or use plastic wrap and tape to seal it.

2 Place a bar magnet on the table and put the container over the magnet. What happens to the iron filings? What kind of shape do the filings make?

3 Lift the container and shake it gently. Face the south pole of two bar magnets end to end about 2 inches (5 cm) apart. Place the container over the magnets. What pattern do the filings form now?

4 Lift the container again and shake it. Try different shaped magnets below the container. What pattern do the filings make when they are placed over a horseshoe magnet? A donut magnet?

What happened?

The iron filings showed the shape of the magnetic field around the magnets. The place where the most filings gathered showed that the areas of strongest attraction are the ends of the bar magnets. The smallest amount of attraction occurs in the middle of the bar magnet. Horseshoe magnets, with the ends nearer to each other, also have the greatest attraction at the ends.

Are the magnet's invisible lines really flat?

You saw the magnetic fields around a magnet in the last activity. These fields looked flat because the surface the filings lay on was level. Is there a way to see how the fields would look in 3D space?

You need

- ◆ adult helper
- ◆ iron filings
- ◆ small clear plastic container with cap
- ◆ baby oil or vegetable oil
- ◆ various magnets, small bar, donut, horseshoe, etc.

Do this

 Have an adult helper place a tablespoon (15 mL) of iron filings into a clear bottle or jar.

2 Pour the oil over the filings and screw the jar lid on very tightly.

3 Rotate the jar several times to mix the filings into the liquid.

4 Hold a magnet next to the jar and look at the pattern created by the filings in the liquid.

5 Move the magnet. Watch what happens to the filings. Try placing different shaped magnets against the side of the container. If you have 2 same-type magnets, place them on opposite sides.

What happened?

The filings didn't arrange themselves in a flat pattern this time. Instead, they formed a pattern in the liquid, fanning out from the sides of the glass. When you added different magnets, the filings moved toward or away from the poles of those magnets and showed the magnetic field in the liquid. The oil allowed the filings to stay suspended for a 3D effect, instead of having gravity pull them flat.

Where is a magnet the strongest ?

Hold a bar magnet in your hand. It isn't heavier at one end than the other. Maybe one end is blue and the other end red, but the surface looks much the same all over. What about strength? Is that the same at both ends? Is it stronger or weaker in the middle? Let's see.

You need

- box of steel paper clips
- bar magnet
- horseshoe magnet
- string
- masking tape

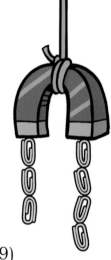

Do this

1. Hang the bar magnet from the string (see pages 8–9) and tape the other end of the string to a table or chair.

2. Attract a single paper clip to the very end of each pole. Attract a second clip to the bottom of the first clip. Keep adding clips until the magnet can't hold any more and the clips fall off.

3 Gather the fallen clips into the box and shake it. Do the activity again, but this time, move the top paper clip closer to the center of the magnet. How many clips can you add before they fall off?

4 What happens at the very center of the magnet? How many paper clips could be held there?

5 Try this activity using a horseshoe magnet. Which part of the magnet attracted the most paper clips? Remember to shake the box of paper clips each time you do this activity.

What happened?

The ends, or poles, of the magnet attracted the most paper clips. This means that the magnetic force was the strongest at the poles. Each end should be the same strength and be able to support the same number of paper clips. You may have found

that the horseshoe magnet held more paper clips than the bar magnet. When the poles of the magnets are close together, it makes the magnet more powerful than if they were farther apart.

What happens if I break a magnet ?

When you drop a glass on the floor, it may shatter and break into many tiny pieces. It would be impossible to put all the pieces back together again so the glass would hold water. But what happens when you break a magnet? Could you still use the pieces?

You need

- ◆ bar magnet
- ◆ thin iron wire, about 1 foot (30 cm) long
- ◆ adult helper
- ◆ steel paper clips
- ◆ nail polish
- ◆ compass
- ◆ wire cutters

Do this

1 Use a bar magnet to stroke the piece of metal wire. Remember, only stroke it in one direction.

2 Hold the metal wire near a paper clip. Does it attract the clip?

3 Place a compass near the wire. Does the compass needle move when it's held near the wire?

4 Have an adult place several dots of nail polish about 3 inches (7.5 cm) apart along the wire. Let the polish dry.

5 Ask your helper to cut the wire at the nail polish spots.

6 Hold the compass near each of the cut wires. Does the needle still move? Use the cut pieces of wire to attract a paper clip. Does the wire still attract the clip? Will the cut wires attract and repel the other pieces of cut wire?

What happened?

Each of the pieces of wire stayed magnetized, even though they had been cut from the long piece of metal. The individual pieces each had a north and a south pole. This is because once the domains in the wire are aligned in the same direction, they will stay that way unless they are disturbed. As long as cutting the wire didn't disturb the domains, you ended up with four shorter magnets instead of one longer magnet.

Are two magnets stronger than one?

If you were playing "tug of war," it would be easier to pull the rope if you had more people on your side. Are magnets stronger if there are more of them working together?

You need

- nonmetallic ruler with groove down length, or two flat rulers
- several bar magnets
- steel ball bearings

Do this

1. Before you begin, hold a bar magnet near a single ball bearing and make sure the bearing is attracted to the magnet.

2 Place the ruler (or two flat rulers side by side to form a groove) someplace level. Put the north pole of the bar magnet next to the end of the ruler. Place the ball bearing in the groove at the 1 inch (2.5 cm) mark. Does the magnet attract the ball bearing? Keep moving the bearing farther away from the magnet. How far can you place the bearing before the magnet doesn't attract it any longer?

3 Put a second bar magnet at the end of the first magnet, with the north pole facing the south pole of the first magnet. Repeat step 2 again. How far can the magnets attract the bearing?

4 Put the second bar magnet over the first bar magnet, with the poles facing the same direction. Repeat step 2 again. Is the magnetic strength greater this time?

What happened?

The more magnets you used in a line, the stronger the attraction. This is because the second magnet adds its magnetic force to the first one. You have more domains aligned in the same direction. When you put the same poles together, they repelled each other, limiting their attraction to the ball bearing.

Can a magnet move things it isn't attracted to?

By now you know what kinds of things a magnet can attract or pick up. This next activity will really confuse you.

You need

♦ small aluminum pie or tart plate
♦ flat, clear plastic container
  or tray
♦ water
♦ strong horseshoe magnet
♦ string

Do this

1. Place the container or tray on a flat surface and fill it with water, nearly to the top. Careful, you don't want to move this container as it might spill.

2. Hold the horseshoe magnet over the aluminum plate. Is the plate attracted to the magnet?

3. Gently float the small plate in the water so it can turn freely.

4 Tie the string ends together. Center the horseshoe magnet in the loop. Spin the magnet around until the string is tightly wound, then hold the magnet over the floating plate. Let the magnet unwind. Watch the plate. What happens to it?

What happened?

Aluminum is not affected by magnets, so at first there was no attraction between the plate and the magnet. But when the magnet was spinning, the plate started to spin in the same direction as the magnet. As the magnet turned, the lines of magnetic force also moved. These force lines hit the plate and caused a small electrical current in the metal. The electricity turned the aluminum plate slightly magnetic, so it was attracted to the turning magnet.

Did You Know?

Magnetic attraction is how an (analog) car speedometer works. A magnet, spun by the wheels, attracts an aluminum plate behind the speedometer. The plate doesn't spin freely; it has a spring attached. The faster the magnet spins, the greater the attraction and the higher the speed on the dial.

Can I make a magnet float in the middle of the air ?

Jump up as high as you can. No matter how hard you try, you don't stay up in the air. Gravity keeps you from flying off the Earth into space. But can you get something to fly?

You need

- ♦ heavy book such as phone directory
- ♦ thread
- ♦ clear tape
- ♦ small donut magnets
- ♦ strong bar magnets
- ♦ box of paper clips

Do this

1 Tape the thread to the cover of the phone directory and place the book on the floor. Tie the other end of the thread through a paper clip.

2. Hold a donut magnet above the paper clip and slowly raise your hand so the clip lifts off the floor and into the air.

3. Keep moving the magnet up in the air until the clip falls back onto the floor. How far above the clip can the magnet be placed before the magnetic attraction no longer works?

4. Try this again, but this time use two donut magnets instead of one. Then try using a bar magnet, then two bar magnets together.

5. Repeat your tests, adding more clips to the string and seeing when they drop away.

What happened?

The clip rose into the air and stayed there as long as you held the donut magnet close enough to the clip for the attraction to work. When you moved the donut magnet too far, the clip fell back to the ground. When you tried to lift more clips, you found that you needed to hold the donut magnet closer to the heavier clips. Using two magnets instead of one added power, lifting a single clip higher and then lifting more clips. The same with the bar magnets. The clips stayed in the air as long as the magnetic force was stronger than the force of gravity.

Can magnets make me laugh?

You've learned the answers to questions you've had about magnets, so it's time to be silly. Try these magnet tricks.

1. Glue a photo of a family member, a famous movie star, or even your pet pooch onto a stiff paper, plastic, or foam plate. Smooth a piece of plastic wrap over the surface of the picture, then sprinkle iron filings onto the plate. Use a magnet under the plate to add bizarre facial features to the pictures (give your sis, or your cat, a mustache).

2. Take a small plastic plate and pile colorful paper clips or metal shapes onto the surface. Put a magnet below it and create tall sculptures.

3 Place magnets under a piece of paper. Sprinkle iron filings on the paper and shake it so the filings reveal the magnetic fields. Use a spray bottle filled with vinegar to lightly wet the filings. Allow the paper to sit undisturbed for several hours. Hang your magnetic pictures.

4 Place two or more donut magnets on a pencil to make a magnetic "spring." Push them together and then let the top one jump off. (Do this over a bed or a carpeted floor. Do this away from breakables.) You can even label the top magnet with heads and tails and do a magnetic coin toss.

5 Draw sea creatures, like fish, starfish, and octopuses, and cut out the pictures. Attach a paper clip to each of the drawings and use a magnet on a string to "fish."

Index